MACMILLAN G
INTERMEC

PHILIP PROWSE

The Woman Who Disappeared

MACMILLAN
ORIGINALS

INTERMEDIATE LEVEL

Series Editor: John Milne

The Macmillan Guided Readers provide a choice of enjoyable reading material for learners of English. The series is published at five levels – Starter, Beginner, Elementary, Intermediate and Upper. At **Intermediate Level**, the control of content and language has the following main features:

Information Control
Information which is vital to the understanding of the story is presented in an easily assimilated manner and is repeated when necessary. Difficult allusion and metaphor are avoided and cultural backgrounds are made explicit.

Structure Control
Most of the structures used in the Readers will be familiar to students who have completed an elementary course of English. Other grammatical features may occur, but their use is made clear through context and reinforcement. This ensures that the reading, as well as being enjoyable, provides a continual learning situation for the students. Sentences are limited in most cases to a maximum of three clauses and within sentences there is a balanced use of simple adverbial and adjectival phrases. Great care is taken with pronoun reference.

Vocabulary Control
There is a basic vocabulary of approximately 1,600 words. Help is given to the students in the form of illustrations, which are closely related to the text.

Contents

1

A Visitor

My name's Samuel. Lenny Samuel. You can call me Len. I'm a private eye. A private eye is a private detective – a detective who will work for anyone who will pay him. I'm not a policeman. I work on my own as a private eye.

My office is on the west side of Los Angeles, on the fourth floor of a high building. There are only two rooms in my office – the outer room and the inner room. The outer room is the waiting-room. There are four chairs in the waiting-room, although there are never four people waiting to see me. In fact, there is usually no one at all waiting to see me.

In the inner room, there's a cheap wooden desk. There's a big wooden chair for me to sit on and, on the opposite side of the desk, there's a low metal chair for my visitors. The rest of the furniture in my office consists of a large, empty metal cupboard, and a low bed in one corner. When there is a lot of work, I sometimes sleep in the office.

The notice outside my door says: "L. Samuel. Private Detective." That's me. I'm quite tall, nearly two metres, and I weigh eighty kilos. A lot of men say that I'm ugly, but women seem to find me attractive. I've got brown eyes, brown hair and very nice teeth. I had a good nose, too, until someone broke it in a fight last year.

Recently, I haven't been very busy. In fact, I've had very little to do. However, I did have some work last month. It all started late one afternoon, when I was sitting in my office. I had just finished cutting my nails and I was about to clean them.

Suddenly, I heard someone walk into the outer room. I always leave the door of the outer room open, in case anyone wants to come in and see me. When I heard the footsteps in the outer room, I wasn't very surprised.

I thought that someone had made a mistake and come into the wrong office. It was probably someone looking for the doctor next door.

But a moment later, there was a very quiet knock on the door of the inner room.

'Come in,' I shouted and put away the scissors I had been cutting my nails with.

The door opened and in walked one of the most beautiful women I had ever seen. She was about eighteen years old, with blue eyes and long blonde hair. She was wearing a smart green coat and had a big brown handbag over her shoulder.

'Excuse me,' said the girl. 'I'm looking for Mr Samuel.'

'I'm Samuel,' I said, with a quick smile. 'Come in and sit down.'

The girl didn't smile back at me.

'No, I won't sit down,' she said.

'Well, if you won't sit down, at least come in and close the door,' I replied.

The girl came in, walked over and put her handbag on my desk.

'Now,' I said, 'what can I do for you?'

'I need help,' said the girl slowly. 'But I don't know if you will be able to help me. Are you a real private detective?'

'Of course I am,' I replied angrily. 'Didn't you see the notice on the office door? It says "L. Samuel. Private Detective." I'm Samuel. I'm a private eye.'

'All right, Mr Samuel,' the girl said coldly. 'There's no need to get angry. I have a little job for you.'

'Right,' I said quickly. 'What do you want me to do?'

'It's very simple really,' the girl replied. 'I want you to find my sister. She has disappeared.'

The door opened and in walked one of the most beautiful women I had ever seen.

2

Please Find My Sister

'I see,' I said. 'Your sister has disappeared. Have you reported her disappearance to the police?'

The blonde girl shook her head. She looked very nervous and was starting to cry.

'No, I haven't told the police,' she said. 'I don't want any trouble with the police. I just want you to help find my sister.'

She took a small, pink handkerchief out of her handbag and dried her eyes.

'All right,' I said. 'Tell me all about your sister.'

'Her name is Elaine Garfield,' said the girl.

'And what's your name?' I interrupted.

'Helen. Helen Garfield,' she replied. 'My sister disappeared a week ago. We had arranged to have dinner together last Monday night, but she didn't come.'

'Perhaps your sister didn't come because she doesn't like the food you cook,' I suggested.

'Don't try to be funny. I flew all the way from New York to see her last Monday,' she said angrily.

'Oh, so you don't live in Los Angeles, then,' I said.

'No,' she replied quickly, 'I live in New York. I flew right across America to see my sister, but, when I got here, I discovered that she had disappeared.'

'How do you know she has disappeared?' I asked. 'Perhaps your sister just forgot about the dinner.'

The blonde girl took a deep breath.

'Look,' she said, 'Let me finish my story. If you don't stop asking questions, I'll find myself another detective.'

'Right,' I said, 'I'm listening.'

'I waited for my sister last Monday evening, in my hotel,' said the girl. 'But she didn't come. I telephoned her, but there was no answer. So the next morning, I went to the office where she worked. At her office, they said that she had been to work the day before, on the Monday. They also told me that she'd left suddenly, in the middle of the afternoon, without telling anyone. After that I went round to her flat, but there was no one there.'

The girl stopped for a minute, and then continued.

'Mr Samuel,' she said, 'I'm very worried about my sister. It's not usual for her to disappear suddenly like this. I'm sure that she's in danger and I want you to find her.'

'All right,' I said. 'It may be easy or it may be difficult, but I'll find her. But first, tell me why you've waited six days before coming to me.'

'That's none of your business,' the girl said.

'OK,' I replied. 'Your sister's name is Elaine Garfield. What does she look like?'

'Oh, that's easy,' Helen Garfield replied, 'she looks like me. We're twins. Now, Mr Samuel, how much money do you charge?'

'Fifty dollars a day,' I said.

'Very well, Mr Samuel,' said the girl, 'but fifty dollars a day is a lot of money. I hope that you will work hard for it.'

'Oh yes,' I replied, with a smile, 'I'll work very hard. Now give me the address of your sister's flat, and the name of the office where she works. I'll start work at once.'

The blonde girl wrote the addresses on a piece of paper and gave me the paper.

'One more thing,' I said. 'Can you give me your address, too?'

'That won't be necessary,' she replied, as she picked up her handbag. 'I'll come and see you again tomorrow afternoon, at five o'clock. Goodbye, Mr Samuel.'

Without waiting for an answer, the girl turned around and walked out of the office.

As I watched her walk out of my office, I smiled to myself.

'This is better than cleaning my nails,' I thought. Then I began my work.

3

The Manson Building

After the blonde girl had left my office, I looked at the two addresses which she had written on the piece of paper. The first was:

Elaine Garfield,
Apartment 716,
Manson Building,
Sunset Place.

The second address was:

Myer and Myer,
Attorneys,
Title-Insurance Building

Putting the paper in my pocket, I got up and walked towards the door. Then I stopped and went back to my desk. I opened the top left-hand drawer and took out my gun, a .38 Smith and Wesson. Then I put the gun back in the drawer. I decided that it was safer to leave it behind. It's easy to get shot, if you're carrying a gun.

I ran down the stairs, all four floors, and out into the street. My old grey Chrysler was outside, so I jumped in and drove off fast, towards Sunset Place.

The Manson Building was a tall, ugly block of apartments. I parked the Chrysler outside and walked towards the big glass front doors.

'Hey, mister!' a voice said.

I continued walking.

'Hey, mister!' said the voice again. 'You can't leave your car there.'

I stopped and turned around. A man in a grey uniform was standing by the Chrysler.

'Hey, mister!' the man repeated, 'you can't park your car here.'

'Why not?' I asked.

'Because only people who live in the Manson Building can park here,' he replied.

'So,' I said, 'How do you know that I don't live in the Manson Building?'

'Because I'm the porter,' the man replied. 'I work in the entrance of the building and let people in and out of the door. I know everybody here.'

'Right,' I said, 'then please let me in.'

The porter and I walked up to the big glass front doors and he let me in.

'Who do you want to see?' the porter asked.

'Miss Elaine Garfield,' I said. 'She lives in Apartment 716.'

'I'm sorry,' the porter replied, 'Miss Garfield is out.'

'When did she go out?' I asked, trying not to look interested.

'Mind your own business,' said the porter. 'I'm not going to tell you. And I'm not going to let you go up to Miss Garfield's apartment, when she's not there.'

'Why don't you go for a walk?' I said to the porter and put five dollars in his hand. I gave the porter the money to make him go away.

The porter shook his head.

'No,' he said.

I gave the porter five dollars more.

'Now go for a long walk,' I said.

The porter went out into the street and I went up to Apartment 716, Miss Elaine Garfield's apartment.

4

A Very Tidy Apartment

I rang the bell beside the door of Apartment 716 and waited. There was no answer. I rang again, but there was still no answer. Then I took a small, square piece of plastic out of my pocket. I looked around. I was alone. I pushed the piece of plastic into the space between the door and the door frame and moved the plastic up and down. In a minute, the door opened and I went into the flat.

I stood still and listened. There was silence. I switched on the light and looked around. It was a modern apartment. I was standing in the living-room. Through an open door on my left, I could see the bedroom which was very neat and tidy. I looked in the wardrobe – it was almost empty.

'That's funny,' I thought. 'People who disappear don't usually take most of their clothes with them. They only take their clothes if they've been planning their disappearance for a long time.'

I walked back into the living-room and searched it carefully. But I found nothing to explain Elaine Garfield's disappearance. Then I went into the kitchen. The kitchen was also very clean and

12

tidy. There were no dirty plates or cups. There was no old milk in the refrigerator. Everything was in its place.

'Well,' I thought, 'there's only the bathroom left to search now.'

The bathroom, too, was empty and clean. I walked quickly around the flat, making sure that I hadn't forgotten anything. I wiped everything I had touched with my handkerchief, because I didn't want to leave any fingerprints. Then I switched off the lights and opened the door to leave.

But I didn't leave. There were two men standing outside the door. One of them was short and had red hair and a nasty smile. The other was quite tall and was wearing a hat pulled down over his face. The one with the hat was holding a gun and the gun was pointing at me.

I tried to close the door, but the red-haired man put his foot out to stop the door closing. I let go of the door. The door opened and both the men came in. The one with the hat was in front and he was still carrying the gun.

'Hold your hands up in the air,' said the man with the gun.

Then he turned to the red-haired man.

'See if he's got a gun on him, Jo.'

Jo, the red-haired man, came over towards me. I waited. When Jo was between me and the man with the gun, I jumped. I jumped forward and caught Jo around the neck. I held him in front of me. The man with the gun couldn't shoot because he would hit his friend.

'Right,' I said to the man with the gun. 'Get out of the way. I'm leaving now and I'm taking your friend with me.'

Holding Jo in front of me, I walked slowly towards the man with the gun. Then something went wrong with my plan.

The man with the gun started to laugh. He put the gun back in his pocket and stood laughing.

'Why are you laughing?' I asked.

13

'I'm laughing because you're so stupid,' the man with the gun said and walked up to me.

'Stop,' I said, 'or else I'll . . .'

'What will you do?' asked the man with the gun. 'You can't do anything. I'm the one with the gun.'

As he said this, the man leant forward. He pulled Jo out of my hands and hit me in the face. I must say that I wasn't expecting to be hit in the face. It hurt. It hurt even more when he hit me again and I fell on the floor. I lay still on the floor, hoping that the two men would go away. But they didn't go away. Instead, they picked me up and hit me hard on the head. Everything went black. I lay on the floor – I was unconscious.

5

Myer and Myer

'I woke up with a terrible pain in my head. I was lying on the floor outside the front door of Miss Elaine Garfield's apartment. I looked around. The man with the gun and his red-haired friend had left. I was alone and I had a terrible headache. I got up slowly and felt my head gently, to see if there was any blood. There wasn't any blood, but my head was still very painful. I decided to go back to the office and go to bed.

There was no sign of the porter at the entrance to the Manson Building. I walked out of the door and across to the old grey Chrysler. I drove slowly back to the office.

The telephone was ringing when I arrived at the office. I went in quickly and answered it.

'Samuel speaking.'

'Listen, Samuel,' replied a voice. 'Forget about Elaine

Garfield. We hurt you a little in her apartment. If you don't forget all about Elaine Garfield, we'll hurt you a lot more.'

'Who are you?' I asked.

But there was no answer. The man had put down the telephone.

I decided to do what the man had told me. I would forget all about Elaine Garfield – for ten hours. After a good night's sleep, I would look for Elaine Garfield. I would also try to find the man with the gun and his friend, Jo. I lay down on the hard, low bed and went straight to sleep.

I woke up the next morning at eight o'clock. I felt my head carefully, but it did not hurt so much now.

I left the office and went across the street to the café where I usually had breakfast. I drank a glass of orange juice, ate some fresh toast and drank several cups of coffee.

I read the morning newspapers. There was a lot of news, but nothing about Miss Elaine Garfield. I looked at my watch, left the café and walked over to the Chrysler.

By nine o'clock, I was outside the Title-Insurance Building. At three minutes past nine, I was standing outside the door of Myer and Myer, Attorneys. At twenty past nine, I was still standing outside the door. Nobody had arrived yet to work. At nine thirty, the first secretary arrived and, at eighteen minutes to ten, I was sitting in Mr Myer's office.

'Well, Mr Myer,' I said, 'my name's Samuel and I'm a private detective.'

'I'm pleased to meet you,' Mr Myer said politely. He was about fifty-five years old, with a grey suit, grey hair and a grey face.

'Does Miss Elaine Garfield work here?' I asked.

'Yes, she does,' Mr Myer said, 'But she hasn't been to work since last Monday. Why do you want to see Elaine?'

'Her sister has asked me to help find her,' I replied. 'Can you think of anything Elaine said or did which could explain her disappearance?'

Mr Myer scratched his head.

'No,' he said, 'I'm afraid I can't help you.'

'Who did Elaine work with?' I asked.

Mr Myer looked at me.

'Why do you say, "Who *did* Elaine work with?" and not "Who *does* Elaine work with?" Elaine's not dead, is she?' he asked.

I looked straight back at Mr Myer.

'I don't know if Elaine is dead or not,' I said. 'Would you be very sad if she was dead?'

'Yes, of course I would be sad!' Mr Myer replied angrily. 'Are you trying to suggest that I know where Elaine is?'

I smiled.

'Now don't get excited, Mr Myer,' I said. 'Can you tell me the name of anyone who works with Elaine – anyone who shares a desk with her or works in the same room?'

'Yes,' Mr Myer said, 'that's easy. Elaine shares a room with Suzy Graham.'

I got up.

'Thank you very much, Mr Myer,' I said. 'Where is Suzy Graham's office, please?'

'It's along the corridor,' said Mr Myer 'the third door on the left.'

I thanked Mr Myer again and walked to the door.

'Oh, Mr Samuel,' Mr Myer said, 'I'm sorry that I got angry, but you understand that I don't want . . .'

'Yes, I understand,' I interrupted. 'You don't want dirty private detectives in your nice, clean office.'

I walked out of Mr Myer's office and banged the door behind me. I walked slowly down the corridor and knocked on the third door on the left.

'Come in,' said a voice.

So I went into the room.

'Are you Suzy Graham?' I asked.

'Yes,' said the girl sitting at the desk. 'I'm Suzy.'

I smiled at her. Suzy, was the kind of girl everyone smiled at. She was small and slim and had a pair of beautiful, brown eyes.

'What can I do to help you?' Suzy asked.

I smiled again.

'I'd like to ask you some questions, Miss Graham.'

'Don't call me Miss Graham,' the girl said, 'you can call me Suzy.'

'Well, Suzy,' I said, 'I would like to ask you some questions about a friend of yours. Her name is Elaine Garfield.'

Suzy stopped smiling.

'Yes, all right,' she said. 'But I don't want to talk about Elaine here in the office.'

'Right,' I replied, 'I'll tell you what we'll do. We'll go out and find a café. I'll buy you a cup of coffee and you can tell me about Elaine. All right?'

Suzy cheered up and looked much happier.

'I'd like to have a cup of coffee,' she said, 'but Mr Myer might get angry if I leave the office.'

'Don't worry about Mr Myer,' I said, with a big smile. 'Mr Myer and I are great friends.'

6

Suzy

Suzy put on her coat and we left the office together. We found a little café, just opposite the Title-Insurance Building.

In the café, I told Suzy why I was asking questions about Elaine Garfield.

'Elaine's twin sister, Helen, thinks that Elaine has disappeared, and she has asked me to find Elaine,' I said. 'Helen told me that she came to Myer and Myer last Tuesday. She was told that Elaine had left work suddenly, last Monday afternoon. Is that right?'

Suzy nodded.

'At least, part of it's right,' she said. 'Elaine was at work last Monday, and she hurried off in the middle of the afternoon.'

Suzy stopped for a minute, and then she continued.

'But I don't remember seeing Elaine's sister, Helen, on Tuesday. In fact, I didn't even know that Elaine had a sister.'

'Elaine's sister lives in New York,' I explained. 'Now, can you remember last Monday afternoon? Did Elaine give any reason for leaving suddenly?'

'Oh, yes,' Suzy said, 'Elaine said that she wasn't feeling well and was going to lie down.'

'Did Elaine receive any visitors or phone calls last Monday afternoon?' I asked.

'No, I don't think so,' said Suzy. 'No wait a minute, I think … yes, Elaine did receive a phone call, just before she left.'

I smiled.

'I don't suppose that, by chance, you might have heard any of the telephone conversation?'

'Certainly not,' Suzy replied, 'I don't listen to other people's phone calls.'

'Can you think of any reason why Elaine disappeared?' I asked.

'No,' Suzy replied, 'Elaine was always very friendly with everyone and she didn't seem to have any troubles.'

'Did Elaine have any special friends, any men or women she talked about a lot?' I asked.

'No, not really,' Suzy replied. 'Elaine and I used to be quite friendly and we went out dancing together a lot. But recently we haven't been out together at all.'

'I understand,' I said, though I really didn't understand anything at all. 'Can you remember the last time you went out together? Can you remember the place you went to?'

'Oh, that's easy,' Suzy said quickly, 'we went to the Las Cabanas Club. We always went there. It was about a month ago. We had an argument there and we haven't gone out together since.'

'What was the argument about?' I asked.

'It was after midnight,' Suzy explained, 'and I wanted to go home. But Elaine said she wanted to stay a bit longer. She said that she had met a wonderful man and didn't want to leave. I said I was going home and I left Elaine in the club. After that evening, one thing led to another.'

'What do you mean,' I asked, ". . . one thing led to another"?'

Suzy smiled.

'I often spoke to Elaine about the man she had met. Elaine thought he was wonderful. I told her that he was no good at all.'

'What did Elaine say when you told her that?' I asked, with interest.

'She became very angry,' replied Suzy. 'We haven't been out dancing together since then.'

I paid for the coffee.

'You've been very helpful, Suzy,' I said, 'and I've only got one more question. Can you remember the name of the man Elaine Garfield met at Las Cabanas?'

'Benny Greep,' Suzy said, 'that's his name. Benny Greep.'

'Thank you very much indeed, Suzy,' I said, with a smile. 'You've been a great help.'

'Not at all,' Suzy said and looked at me with her beautiful, big, brown eyes. 'If there's anything else I can do for you, just ask.'

I looked straight into her eyes.

'What are you doing tonight?' I asked.

'I'll be at home watching television,' Suzy replied. 'My boyfriend's a boxer and he's fighting in a match on television tonight.'

'Goodbye, Suzy,' I said and watched her as she walked back across the street to the Tide-Insurance Building. Her boyfriend was a boxer! That was just my luck.

7

Benny Greep

I looked at my watch. It was nearly eleven o'clock. I went back into the café and asked if I could look at the telephone book. I turned to "L" and ran my finger down the outside of the page. Soon, I found the name I was looking for: "Las Cabanas". I looked more closely. The address was:

Las Cabanas, 232 Golden Drive. Telephone: 323.0313

I left the café and walked over to where I had parked the Chrysler. It wasn't time for lunch yet, so I decided to go and see what Las Cabanas was like. It took me nearly twenty minutes to drive there and another ten minutes to find somewhere to park.

Have you ever seen a night club in the daytime? It's a very depressing sight. At night, a nightclub seems wonderful. However, at a quarter to twelve in the moming, it looks old, empty and dirty. The man I met at Las Cabanas looked old, empty and dirty, too.

I rang the bell for five minutes before he answered the door. Even then, he didn't open the door itself. Instead, he opened a small window in the door.

'What do you want?' he asked. 'The club doesn't open until ten o'clock tonight.'

'I'm looking for someone,' I said, 'someone called Benny Greep.'

'I don't know anyone called Benny Greep,' the man replied and started to shut the window.

'Wait a minute,' I said and pushed five dollars through the window.

'That's better,' the man said.

And he opened the door and let me in.

I followed him across the dance floor. The man was a cleaner. He picked up a brush and began to clean the floor.

'Do you know where I can find Benny Greep?' I asked the man again.

'If you come back tonight at ten o'clock, you'll find Benny Greep here,' the man said. 'Benny plays the drums in the band.'

I gave the man another five dollars.

'Where can I find Benny now?' I asked.

The man picked up a piece of paper from the floor and wrote an address on it.

I took the paper and left immediately.

As I drove the grey Chrysler away from Las Cabanas, I looked at the address the cleaner had written:

5314 ARVIEDA STREET
WEST LOS ANGELES

5314 Arvieda Street was an old block of apartments. I gave the porter a couple of dollars and he told me which was Benny Greep's apartment. I walked up the narrow, dark stairs until I came to the fifth floor. I was looking for Apartment 507.

I knocked on the door of Apartment 507 and waited. There was no answer, so I rang the bell. No answer. I knocked again, hard. There was still no answer.

I pushed against the door and it opened easily. I waited. There was no sound from the apartment, so I went in. The light was on and the curtains were drawn. The apartment was very small. There was one main room, which was used as the living-room, dining-room and bedroom. The room had two doors. One of the doors led into the kitchen and the other into the bathroom.

The main room was very untidy. The table was covered with dirty plates and glasses and there was a full ashtray lying on the floor. There was a strange smell in the room.

I looked into the kitchen. The kitchen was also dirty and untidy. I walked across to the bathroom and opened the door.

Benny Greep was in the bath. His left hand was hanging over

the side of the bath. The hand had neatly cut nails, and there was a gold ring on one finger. The wrist was covered by a shirt-sleeve, which was rather dirty. I couldn't see the rest of the arm, because it was under the water.

Benny Greep's head was just out of the water. He had a handsome face and quite long, black hair. His eyes were wide open. The only other parts of his body out of the water were his feet. But I couldn't see his toes because he still had his shoes and socks on. The bath water was red.

I pulled out the plug in the bath, to let the water out. When the bath was empty, I looked at the dead man more closely. He had been dead for several hours. He had been shot in the chest and then pushed into the bath. I looked on the floor by the bath. There was blood there, too, and I was standing in it. I moved back and cleaned the blood off my shoes with some water.

Then I quickly looked round the main room again. The dead man's coat was lying on a chair and I felt in the pockets. I found a few dollars and a driving licence. The driving licence had a photograph of the dead man on it. The licence belonged to Benny Greep, and the address in the licence was 5314 Arvieda Street, West Los Angeles. The dead man in the bath was definitely Benny Greep.

Arrested for Murder

I moved around the room and carefully cleaned everything I had touched. I didn't want to leave any fingerprints. There was nothing in the room to connect Benny Greep with Elaine Garfield. I picked up the telephone and asked for the police.

'I'm speaking from Apartment 507, 5314 Arivieda Street,' I said. 'There's a dead man in the bath.'

'Right,' said the policeman at the other end of the telephone. 'What's your name?'

I told him.

'Don't touch anything,' the policeman said, 'and stay where you are. A police car will be there in a few minutes.'

I put down the phone and sat down to wait. Three minutes later, I heard the police car coming. The car stopped outside the building and I could hear heavy feet running up the stairs.

Two policemen walked into the apartment. They were both wearing ordinary clothes and looked hot and tired. One was about twenty-five years old, the other about forty.

The older policeman came up to me and showed me his police papers.

'Where's the body?' he asked.

I pointed to the bathroom. Both policemen went into the bathroom to have a look. The younger one came back first, shaking his head.

'All right,' said the younger policeman, 'why did you do it?'

'Do what?' I asked in surprise.

'Why did you kill your friend in the bath?' said the young policeman.

'He wasn't my friend,' I replied.

'I don't care if he was your friend or not,' said the policeman. 'Tell me why you killed, him.'

'I didn't kill him,' I said calmly.

'Then what are you doing here?' asked the older policeman, coming in from the bathroom.

'My name's Lenny Samuel,' I explained. 'I'm a private detective and I came here to talk to Benny Greep. The door was open and so I came in. I looked in the bathroom and I found the dead man in the bath, so I telephoned the police. The dead man is Benny Greep.'

'Why did you want to talk to Benny Greep?' the younger policeman asked.

'I'm sorry, I can't answer that,' I replied.

'Who are you working for?' asked the older policeman.

'I'm sorry, I can't answer that either,' I said. 'As far as I know, Benny Greep's death doesn't have anything to do with the person I'm working for.'

'Tell me who you are working for,' shouted the younger policeman angrily.

'Take it easy,' said the older policeman to the younger one. 'You stay here until the other police arrive. I'm going to take Mr Samuel down to the police station.'

I kept quiet and followed the older policeman out of the room and down the stairs. Outside the building, we got into my old Chrysler. The policeman drove. We were soon at the police station, where the policeman locked me in a small room. I sat down on a hard, wooden chair in the locked room and tried to sleep.

It was no use getting angry or upset at being arrested for murder. That is something you have to get used to, if you are a private detective. It happens all the time.

But I could not sleep. I was thinking about all the things which had happened since I had met Helen Garfield the day before. I couldn't sleep, because several things were worrying me. But I couldn't remember what those things were.

Sergeant Murphy

While I was in the police station, I remembered one of th
things which was worrying me. How had Jo and his tal
friend known that I was in Elaine Garfield's apartment? Th
porter at the Manson Building must have told the two men.
decided that I would go and talk to the porter when I left the polic
station.

I sat back in the chair and looked at my watch. The time wa
nearly four o'clock.

Then I remembered that Helen Garfield was coming to m
office at five o'clock. I would not be there to meet her.

But there was something else that was worrying me. It wasn'
anything important. It was quite a small thing. But I couldn'
remember what it was.

Suddenly, the door opened and a policeman came in.

'Stand up,' shouted the policeman. 'Follow me.'

I stood up and followed the policeman out of the room an
along a corridor. The policeman stopped, knocked on a door an
opened it.

'Are you ready to see the private detective?' asked the police
man, as he put his head around the door.

Without waiting for an answer, the policeman opened th
door wide and pushed me into the room. The policeman cam
into the room and closed the door behind him.

In the room, there was a man sitting behind a desk. He wa
completely bald – he had no hair at all. He was about fifty-fiv
years old and his name was Sergeant Murphy. Sergeant Murph
had spent all his life in the police and he didn't like privat
detectives.

Sergeant Murphy sat looking at me. He looked at me fo

about five minutes, without saying anything. I was standing in front of his desk, looking straight back at him. The silence didn't worry me. In fact, I quite liked it. The silence was much nicer than questions about what I'd been doing in Benny Greep's apartment.

'What were you doing in Benny Greep's apartment?' asked Sergeant Murphy suddenly. .

'I wanted to talk to him,' I replied.

'Why did you kill Benny Greep?' shouted Sergeant Murphy suddenly.

'I didn't kill him,' I replied, and I told Sergeant Murphy the same story that I had told the policemen in Benny Greep's apartment.

'I don't believe a word of what you've told me,' said the sergeant. 'Who are you working for?'

'I'm sorry,' I replied, 'I can't tell you who I'm working for. As far as I know, Benny Greep's death has nothing to do with me or with the person I'm working for.'

I stopped and looked at the sergeant. I knew that what I had just said wasn't true. In fact, I thought Benny Greep's death was connected with Elaine Garfield's disappearance. But I couldn't tell the police. Helen Garfield had said that she didn't want the police to know about her sister's disappearance.

Sergeant Murphy looked me straight in the eyes.

'I hate all private detectives,' he said slowly, 'and you are the private detective that I hate the most. I don't think you are telling me the truth. I think you are hiding things from me. I think you know more about Benny Greep's death than you say you do. And you are going to tell me all you know – *now*.'

'I've already told you all I know,' I replied quietly.

Sergeant Murphy's face went red. The red colour went up until it covered all of his bald head.

'I hate all private detectives,' he said slowly, 'and you are the private detective I hate the most.'

'Don't try to play, games with me,' he shouted. 'Now get out.'

'Can I go home now?' I asked.

'No,' said Sergeant Murphy.

The sergeant told the policeman at the door to take me back to the small room and lock me up again.

I went with the policemen and didn't argue. I don't like arguing with policemen. When I was alone in the room again, I sat down. I tried to remember the other thing that had been worrying me earlier. Someone had said something important, but I could not remember what it was.

10

The Yellow Car

I looked at my watch. It was half past five. I was still at the police station. I'd seen Sergeant Murphy once more, during the afternoon. It hadn't been a pleasant meeting. I hadn't told the sergeant who I was working for. And I hadn't told him why I'd wanted to talk to Benny Greep.

Half past five. I wondered if Helen Garfield was waiting for me at my office.

Suddenly, the door of the room opened and Sergeant Murphy came in.

'Get out,' he said, 'I've decided to let you go. Now go before I change my mind.'

I went before Sergeant Murphy changed his mind. As I got my car out of the police garage, I wondered why Sergeant Murphy had let me go.

As I drove away from the police station, I noticed a small yellow car behind me. A minute later, I looked in the mirror again. The small yellow car was still behind me. I drove a little faster and then suddenly turned right up a narrow street. At the end of the narrow street, I turned left and then left again. Soon, I was back on the main road. I looked in the mirror. The yellow car was still right behind me.

So that was why Sergeant Murphy had let me go. The sergeant had ordered some policemen to follow me. They were going to watch what I did and who I met.

I drove straight back to the office. As I parked the car outside, I noticed the yellow car had stopped across the road. I ran up the stairs and into my office. The door to the outer room was open, as usual, but the room was empty.

Helen Garfield wasn't, there. But there was a letter on the table, on top of the magazines. I picked the letter up and read it.

> Dear Mr. Samuel,
> I came here at five o'clock and waited but you didn't come. I must see you urgently. Meet me at Las Cabanas at 11.30 tonight.
>
> Helen Garfield.

I put the letter in my pocket and looked at my watch. It was just after six o'clock. I had five and a half hours before the meeting with Helen Garfield. There was plenty of time to go to the Mansion Building and talk to the porter. I got into the Chrysler and drove off towards the Mansion Building. The small yellow car was still following me. As I drove, I thought about Helen Garfield's letter.

'Why does she want to meet me at Las Cabanas?' I asked myself. 'In fact, how does she know about Las Cabanas at all? She says that she lives in New York.'

I would have to ask Miss Helen Garfield a few questions, the next time I saw her.

But the most important thing now was to get away from the yellow car, which was still following me. I was going to the building where Elaine Garfield lived and I didn't want the police to know.

There were two men in the yellow car. I turned right and the yellow car followed. I stopped and the yellow car stopped. I turned the Chrysler around and the yellow car turned around. I tried to drive faster than the yellow car, but the Chrysler was too old and too slow.

I slowed down and waited until I was near the next traffic lights. Then, just as the lights were changing from green to red, I drove across them. The yellow car was too late. The lights were now red. But that didn't stop the car. It drove straight past the red light.

Then, as I looked angrily in my mirror, something happened which made me laugh. A policeman on a motorbike drove after the yellow car. The policeman made the driver stop, because he had driven past the red light.

I drove away as fast as possible. In my mirror, I could see the driver inside the car arguing with the policeman on the motorbike. It was the funniest sight I had seen for a long time. I drove on towards the Manson Building, happy to have escaped. I may even have sung a little, because I was feeling so good.

11

A Short Visit to the Manson Building

As I was driving happily towards the Manson Building, I had a surprise. I looked in the mirror. The yellow car was coming up fast behind me.

I drove as fast as I could, but the yellow car got closer and closer. Just then, a dog ran across the road, in front of the Chrysler. I braked hard and the tyres screamed as the Chrysler stopped suddenly to avoid the dog. Then there was the scream of more tyres as the driver of the yellow car tried to stop.

There was a loud crash and a bang, as the small yellow car ran right into the back of my big, old, grey Chrysler. The two men in the yellow car weren't hurt, but their car was badly damaged and

A policeman on a motorbike drove after the yellow car. The
policeman made the driver stop.

the front. Oil and water were running out onto the road. The old Chrysler was not damaged at all. I got out and walked back to the yellow car.

'You ought to be more careful,' I said to the driver. 'You were driving very dangerously. It's lucky for you that my car isn't badly damaged.'

'But . . . but . . . ,' the driver began to say, but I did not wait to listen.

I ran back to the Chrysler, jumped in and drove on. The last I saw of the yellow car was the two men pushing it to the side of the road.

I was soon at the Manson Building and I went into the hall, to look for the porter. I couldn't see him anywhere. Then I noticed a door with a sign on it saying "Porter". I knocked quietly, but there was no answer. I opened the door slowly and looked into the room.

The porter was sitting at his desk, asleep. His feet were on the desk and he was lying back in his chair. I walked quickly and quietly into the room and closed the door. I went up to the desk and noticed a piece of paper lying by the telephone. There was a telephone number written on the paper – 323.0313.

'Las Cabanas,' I said to myself. 'That's the telephone number of the nightclub.'

Without waking the porter, I left the room. I had found out what I wanted to know. The two men who had hit me on the head had probably come from Las Cabanas. The porter must have telephoned them when I went up to Elaine Garfield's flat.

I was now very interested in Las Cabanas. Elaine Garfield used to go dancing there with Suzy. Benny Greep worked there before he was killed. Helen Garfield wanted to meet me there at half past eleven. And now the porter and the two men who had hit me on the head were connected with Las Cabanas.

I went home, washed, changed and had a meal. At eleven o'clock, I went out again. I was going to Las Cabanas.

There were lots of cars parked outside and I had to leave the Chrysler quite a long way away from the nightclub. As I walked up to the entrance of Las Cabanas, it started to rain heavily. I knocked on the door and the little window in the door opened. A face looked at me for a minute. Then the door opened and I went in. The club no longer looked empty and dirty. Soft lights and sweet music had changed the appearance of the club completely. I stood and looked around. There was a small dance floor, on which a few people were dancing.

The band was small and not very good. There was a new drummer instead of Benny Greep. Around the dance floor, several groups of people were sitting round low tables. To the right of the dance floor, there were more tables where people were eating. There were two doors behind the tables, which led into the kitchen. I sat down at a table by the dance floor, in the darkest part of the room, and waited.

12

Las Cabanas

Exactly at eleven thirty, Helen Garfield came into the night-club. She was looking as beautiful as ever, but seemed to be a little worried. Her blue eyes looked around the room until she saw me. Then, with a little smile, she walked up and sat down at the table. She sat next to me, with her back to the dance floor. She was carrying a bag, which she put on the floor beside her. The smile disappeared from her face.

'Where were you this afternoon, Mr Samuel?' she said sharply. 'I'm paying you fifty dollars a day. In return for that money, I want you to do what I tell you. Now why weren't you at your office this afternoon at five o'clock?'

She was looking as beautiful as ever, but seemed to be a little worried.

I took a deep breath.

'Well, Miss Garfield,' I said, 'it's a long story. Let's have a drink and I'll tell you all about it.'

A waiter came over and I ordered some drinks.

When the waiter had gone, the beautiful, blonde girl said, 'Come on, Mr Samuel, tell me.'

'OK,' I said, 'but stop calling me Mr Samuel. Call me Len – all my friends call me Len.'

'I'm not a friend of yours, Mr Samuel,' the blonde girl said, in a voice like ice. 'I'm paying you a lot of money to work for me.'

'Fifty dollars a day doesn't allow you to be rude to me,' I replied quietly. 'In the last twenty four hours, I've been hit on the head and suspected of murder.'

'What do you mean?' the girl said, and leant towards me. 'Murder?'

Just then, the waiter brought the drinks and we sat in silence until he had gone. Then I told Helen Garfield about my visit to her sister's apartment in the Manson Building. I told her about the two men who had caught me there. Helen Garfield listened in silence.

'Do you like the band, Miss Garfield?' I asked.

'I didn't come here to talk about the band,' the blonde girl said angrily.

'The band has got a new drummer tonight,' I said, 'because I found the old drummer dead in his bath this morning.'

The blonde girl turned around quickly to look at the band. She said something to herself which I didn't hear. She lifted her right hand and started stroking her hair. She looked sad and very worried.

'What . . . what was the drummer . . . the dead man's name?' Helen Garfield asked.

'Greep,' I said, 'Benny Greep. I don't suppose that you know Benny Greep, do you?'

Helen Garfield shook her head.

'No,' she said.

I told her what had happened at the police station. Then I told her about the policemen who had followed me in a yellow car.

'Do you think they're still following you?' the blonde girl asked quickly and looked around the club.

I told her how I had got away from the yellow car.

'Now, Miss Garfield,' I continued, 'it's time for me to ask you a few questions. There are some things about your sister's disappearance which worry me. I want to ask you about them.'

'All right,' she said, 'but I don't think I can help you. I don't know much about Elaine's life here. I don't know very much about Los Angeles, either.'

I sat back in my chair and looked at her. This beautiful, blonde girl was paying me fifty dollars a day to find her sister. I liked what I saw. Then, very quietly, I began to ask Helen Garfield some questions.

'You don't know Los Angeles very well?' I began.

'That's right,' the girl replied.

'But you were able to find out where Elaine worked,' I continued. 'And you went to Myer and Myer last Tuesday, to ask if they knew anything about Elaine.'

'Yes,' the girl said, looking at me closely.

'Who did you speak to at Myer and Myer?' I asked. 'Suzy?'

'No,' the girl said, 'I spoke to Mr Myer.'

'I want to ask you something else,' I said. 'When I went to Elaine's flat, I noticed something unusual. There were very few clothes in the wardrobe. It seems your sister planned her disappearance quite carefully. She had taken her clothes with her.'

'I see,' the girl said and looked around the nightclub.

I waited until she looked back at me.

'Do you like it here?' I asked.

'Yes,' she said.

'I like it, too,' I said, 'But there's something else which is worrying me. Do you mind if I ask you one more question?'

'Not at all,' the girl said.

'Well,' I began, 'I've been wondering why you asked me to meet you here, at Las Cabanas.'

Helen Garfield pushed back her chair and stood up.

'Would you please excuse me for a minute?' she said.

She picked her bag up from the floor and walked over towards the ladies' toilet, which was near the entrance.

'Would you like another drink?' I shouted after her.

'Yes, please,' she shouted back, over her shoulder. I ordered two more drinks and sat back in my chair. I looked around the nightclub. It was almost midnight.

13

Helen Garfield Leaves

I sat by the dance floor in Las Cabanas, waiting for Helen Garfield to come back from the toilet. I was waiting for her to answer my question. I wanted to know why she had asked me to meet her here. I looked around at the people who were dancing.

On the other side of the dance floor, I could see people sitting eating at the tables. Waiters were carrying food in and out of the two doors leading to the kitchen.

I looked at my watch again. It was five past twelve. Helen Garfield was taking a long time. I finished my drink and ordered another one.

At ten past twelve, I got up and walked over towards the entrance. There was a man standing by the front door of the nightclub. I asked him if he had seen Helen.

'The beautiful blonde with blue eyes?' the man asked.

'Yes,' I said.

'She left nearly a quarter of an hour ago,' said the man.

'Are you sure?' I asked.

'Yes,' the man replied. 'She asked me to get her a taxi.'

'Did you hear her give the taxi driver an address?' I asked quickly.

The man shook his head.

'No,' he said, 'I'm sorry.'

I thanked the man and walked back to my seat.

Why did Helen Garfield leave without telling me? I asked myself. Perhaps some of the questions that I asked made her angry.

Just then, I looked up and saw a man walking across the dance floor towards me. I recognised the man. He was short, with red hair. He was looking at me and smiling in a rather unfriendly way. It was Jo – one of the men who had found me in Elaine Garfield's apartment.

I decided to leave. I stood up and started to walk towards the door. I didn't want to meet Jo again. As I walked towards the door, I thought that I heard someone shouting.

'Excuse me, sir,' said a voice.

I didn't stop or look around. Then I heard the voice again.

'Excuse me, sir. You haven't paid your bill.'

I had forgotten to pay for the drinks. The waiter came running up to me and I quickly took out ten dollars and gave them to the waiter.

'You can keep the change,' I said as I gave him the money.

Without waiting for a reply, I turned and hurried towards the door.

Then I heard the waiter's voice again.

'Excuse me, sir, excuse me, sir,' he said.

I stopped and turned around. The waiter came up to me.

'Excuse me, sir, ten dollars is not enough,' he said, 'The price of your drinks is twelve dollars.'

'Las Cabanas is very expensive,' I said, as I gave the waiter another five dollars. 'Now, you can keep the change.'

Then I stopped thinking about money. Jo was walking quickly towards me. I turned around and ran towards the door as fast as I could. I got to the door and was just about to leave Las Cabanas. I was happy because I had escaped.

Then I got a surprise. There, standing by the door of the nightclub, was Jo's tall friend. It was the same man who had hit me on the head in Miss Garfield's apartment. The tall man had seen me coming and had moved in front of the door. Now, I couldn't get out.

14

The Fight

I stopped and looked behind me. Jo was closer now and the smile on his face looked very unfriendly. I was caught. I could not go out of the door and Jo was right behind me.

I turned around quickly and ran towards Jo. Before he knew what I was doing, I put my arms around him and started dancing. He was very surprised and tried to pull away from me. But he couldn't fight properly. He was afraid that the other people would notice.

I looked over my shoulder and saw the tall man standing helplessly on the side of the dance floor. I pushed Jo into the middle of the dance floor, where there were lots of other people dancing.

Then I felt something sharp touching my back. It was a knife.

'Stop trying to be funny, Samuel,' said Jo angrily. 'Stop dancing and go over to the door or else I'll push this knife into you.'

We were right in the middle of the dance floor and a long way from the tall man. Jo was holding a knife against my back. Some of the other people around us had stopped dancing. They were staring in surprise at the sight of two men dancing together.

I lifted my foot and kicked Jo's leg as hard as I could. He gave a cry of pain and fell to the floor. I looked around to see where I could run to. Jo's tall friend was coming through the dancers towards me.

I turned around and ran off the dance floor. I looked back over my shoulder and saw that both Jo and his friend were following me.

I ran between the tables where people were eating. The floor was slippery and I fell over. As I fell, I knocked over a table and the plates of food and glasses fell on top of me.

I got up quickly and ran out through one of the doors into the kitchen. Then I stopped and counted to five.

As Jo and his tall friend were coming towards the door, I pushed the door closed as hard as I could. There was a loud bang as the men ran into the door.

I smiled and turned round. But I did not smile for very long. Three cooks were coming towards me with big kitchen knives in their hands.

I looked at the cooks and at the knives they were holding. I thought about running towards them and trying to fight them. I decided that it would be a stupid idea to try and fight three big men with knives.

To my left, there was a very big saucepan full of boiling soup on the stove. I picked it up and threw it at the cooks. There were loud cries of pain as the hot soup hit the three men.

Just then, the door opened behind me. Jo and his tall friend stood in the doorway, and the tall man was holding a gun.

There was a loud bang as the gun went off. The bang was followed by a scream of pain from one of the cooks, because the tall man had shot him in the foot by mistake.

I quickly picked up a large pile of dirty plates and threw them at Jo. He saw the plates coming and he tried to move away. As

I quickly picked up a large pile of dirty plates and threw them at Jo.

he moved, he slipped on the floor and fell onto a pile of broken plates.

Without waiting, I ran to a door at the back of the kitchen. The door was locked and I banged against the door with my shoulder. The lock broke easily and I pushed the door open. As I ran out into the dark street, I could still hear the shouts and cries coming from the Club.

I came to the Chrysler and bent over to open the door. Just then, there was a noise behind me. I turned around and saw a man with his arm raised. Then I felt a terrible pain in my head. Everything went black. I fell to the ground, unconscious.

15

The Police Station

'Feeling better now?' asked a voice.

I opened my eyes and looked around me. I didn't know where I was. I was lying on something hard and there was a bright light on my eyes.

'Where am I?' I asked.

Then I realised where I was. I recognised the grey walls, the hard furniture and the bright electric lights. I was in the police station again.

'Feeling better now?' the voice repeated.

I looked at the policeman who was talking to me.

'Yes,' I said very slowly, 'but my head feels as if it is breaking in half.'

'You're lucky to be alive,' said the policeman. 'A police car found you lying in the middle of the road on Golden Drive. You would have been hit by passing cars – and probably killed, if the police car hadn't found you.'

I thought for a moment. I wasn't sure how much the police knew. I didn't want to tell the police anything they did not already know.

'Yes, I was lucky,' I said. 'By the way, what was a police car doing on Golden Drive?'

'Oh,' said the policeman, 'there was a big fight at a nightclub called Las Cabanas. We had a telephone call to say that there was a madman in the club. The madman was breaking up all the furniture. A police car was sent to the nightclub, but the madman escaped before the police arrived. The police car was returning when it found you lying in the middle of the road. You were very lucky. The car nearly ran right over you.'

I smiled.

'I don't feel very lucky,' I replied. 'In fact, I feel terrible.'

'Never mind,' said the policeman. 'Can you walk?'

I stood up and walked a few steps. My head hurt, but otherwise I felt all right.

'Yes,' I said, 'I can walk.'

'Good,' the policeman said, 'let's walk along the corridor, then, and have a talk with a friend of yours.'

We went along the corridor. The policeman stopped at a door and knocked. There was a shout from inside the room and the policeman opened the door. I walked into the room and the policeman followed. He shut the door and stood in front of it.

There was only one desk in the room and behind the desk was a man. He was bald. It was my 'old friend', Sergeant Murphy.

'Hello, Sergeant Murphy,' I said, trying to smile. 'How are you feeling tonight?'

Sergeant Murphy didn't smile back at me.

'Are you trying to be funny?' he asked. 'It isn't night, it's morning. You've been unconscious all night.'

'Oh,' I said.

'Now,' said Sergeant Murphy, 'let's begin. I want you to tell me why you were lying, unconscious, in the middle of Golden Drive at half past twelve last night. You were a danger to the traffic.'

'I thought that the traffic was a danger to me,' I replied. But the sergeant didn't even smile.

'I'm waiting for you to tell me what happened,' said the sergeant.

'Nothing much happened,' I began, 'I spent part of the evening at Las Cabanas and left just before midnight. I walked back to my car. Just as I was about to get into the car, someone hit me over the head. That's the last I remember.

'This policeman,' and I pointed to the one standing by the door, 'told me that I had been found in the middle of the road. Someone must have put me there.'

Sergeant Murphy smiled.

'Yes,' he said, 'someone who wanted to kill you put you in the middle of the road. Someone was hoping that a car would hit you and kill you.'

I smiled back at the sergeant.

'Can you think of anyone who would want to kill you?' the sergeant asked me.

'Oh, yes,' I replied, 'hundreds of people would like to kill me, including a few policemen.'

16

Tell Me the Truth

'Did you leave Las Cabanas before midnight?' asked Sergeant Murphy.

'That's right,' I replied, 'I left the nightclub just before twelve.'

'So you weren't at Las Cabanas when the big fight started, just after twelve?' asked the sergeant.

'Big fight?' I said, trying to sound surprised.

'Don't sound so surprised,' said Sergeant Murphy angrily. 'We received a telephone call from the owner of Las Cabanas. He said that just after midnight last night, a tall man with brown hair and brown eyes, called Lenny Samuel, attacked two of the people

47

at the club. The owner of the club said that you 'then attacked and injured three cooks. Then you broke over one hundred plates and a table, and ruined food worth several hundred dollars.'

I didn't say anything. I could not think of anything to say.

'Did you really do all that?' Sergeant Murphy asked, in a different voice. The Sergeant sounded both surprised and pleased. 'Did you really do all that on your own, or did you have men to help you?'

'I did it all on my own,' I said, beginning to feel a little proud of myself.

'Do you know that you could go to prison for six months for what you did last night?' the sergeant asked. He was laughing as he said it.

I wasn't laughing. I couldn't see anything funny about six months in prison.

'Look,' Sergeant Murphy said, 'I'm not stupid.'

I agreed with the sergeant that he was not stupid.

'I'm not stupid,' Sergeant Murphy repeated, 'and I know why you were at Las Cabanas last night. Benny Greep used to work there and you went to find out about his death.'

I agreed with the sergeant again. It seemed the best thing to do.

'Now,' Sergeant Murphy said slowly, 'I'm interested in Las Cabanas. The club is owned by people who are criminals. But we can't prove that they have broken the law. I'm also interested in Benny Greep's murder. Now, what I suggest is this. Tell me all you know about Las Cabanas and Benny Greep and I will let you go. If you tell me all you know, you won't go to prison for the fight at the nightclub. But I want the truth, not the lies you told me yesterday.'

I took a deep breath and started to tell the sergeant what I knew. I told him about everything except Elaine Garfield. I wasn't sure how closely Elaine Garfield was connected with Benny Greep's death. So, I told the sergeant that Helen Garfield, from New York, had asked me to find out about Las Cabanas.

Sergeant Murphy asked me for Helen Garfield's address in New York and I said I didn't know it. Then the sergeant asked me where Helen Garfield was staying in Los Angeles. I said I didn't know.

I told Sergeant Murphy all that I knew about Benny Greep, except that the drummer had known Elaine Garfield. Then I asked him about the two men in the yellow car, who had followed me. The sergeant smiled and said that the two men were policemen. Finally, I told him about the fight at Las Cabanas.

Sergeant Murphy listened to everything. When I had finished my story, he looked at me in silence for a few moments.

'Right, Samuel, I hope that you've told me the truth, and all the truth. If you've been telling me more lies, I'll make sure that you go to prison for six months, because of the fight at Las Cabanas. Now, you can go.'

I stood up.

'Thank you,' I said, with a smile.

'Sit down,' he said, 'and listen. You can go. But you must promise to tell me anything you find out about Las Cabanas and about Benny Greep.'

'I promise,' I said quickly and stood up.

'Wait a minute,' said Sergeant Murphy. 'I've one more thing to tell you. I'm going to telephone the New York police. I'm going to ask them to find out all they can about Helen Garfield. If the police in New York discover that you've told me lies about Helen Garfield, you will be in very serious trouble.'

I told the sergeant not to worry and thanked him very much. I left the police station feeling very happy because Sergeant Murphy had let me go. I called a taxi and went out to Golden Drive to get the Chrysler.

17

Telephone Calls

I drove the Chrysler back to the office and walked up the stairs. The office looked just the same. There were no letters for me. I went down to the café and had a late breakfast. As I drank my coffee, I thought about some of the things Helen Garfield had told me at Las Cabanas before the fight.

I decided to check one of the things immediately and walked over to the telephone. I opened the telephone book and looked under 'M' until I found the telephone number of Myer and Myer. I picked up the telephone and dialled the number.

'Myer and Myer, good morning,' said a voice which I recognised. 'Can I help you?'

'Hello, Suzy,' I said, 'this is Len Samuel. Do you remember me?'

'Of course I remember you,' said Suzy.

'Did your boyfriend win his boxing match on television?' I asked.

'No,' Suzy replied, 'and anyway, he's not my boyfriend any more.'

'Really,' I said happily, thinking that perhaps I could ask Suzy to go for a drink with me.

'Yes,' Suzy said, 'the boxer had a fight with my new boyfriend outside my house last night.'

'And who won?' I asked.

'My new boyfriend,' replied Suzy.

'Oh,' I said sadly, 'and what does your new boyfriend do?'

'My new boyfriend's a weight lifter.' Suzy replied. 'He lifts big weights in competitions.'

I was about to say goodbye. Then I remembered that I had

not telephoned to speak to, Suzy. I wanted to speak to her boss, Mr Myer.

'Can I speak to Mr Myer please, Suzy?' I asked.

'Right,' Suzy said, 'I'll put you through to Mr Myer. Goodbye.'

There was a pause and then I heard Mr Myer's voice.

'Hello, Myer speaking.'

'Good morning Mr Myer,' I said, in a deep voice. I had put my handkerchief over the telephone, so that Mr Myer would not know my voice.

'This is the police,' I said, 'Sergeant Murphy speaking.'

I pretended to be Sergeant Murphy so that Mr Myer would answer my questions.

'Good morning,' said Mr Myer. 'What do you want to ask me about?'

'It's about a girl who works for you,' I said. 'Her name is Elaine Garfield. She has disappeared and we are trying to find her. Elaine's sister, Helen, came to see you last Tuesday, didn't she?'

'No,' said Mr Myer, 'Elaine's sister didn't come to see me last Tuesday. I didn't know that Elaine had a sister, until a private detective told me. He said that Elaine's sister was called Helen.'

The telephone line was very bad and it was difficult for me to hear what Mr Myer was saying.

'What did you say?' I asked.

'I said that Elaine's sister was called Helen,' replied Mr Myer. 'The names are very similar, aren't they?'

'Thank you very much, Mr Myer,' I said and put the telephone down.

Mr Myer was right. The names Helen and Elaine were very similar. Elaine Garfield had disappeared. And so far, I was the only person who had met Helen Garfield.

I left the café and walked back up to my office. As I climbed the stairs, I could hear my telephone ringing. I didn't hurry. I walked slowly along the corridor into my office, and answered the telephone.

'Is that Samuel?' a voice said. I recognised the voice at once. It was Jo.

'Yes,' I said, 'this is Len Samuel.'

'Listen, Samuel,' Jo said, 'we want Elaine Garfield and we think you know where she is. We are coming to your office to see you. Wait for us. Don't go out.'

'But I . . .' I started, but it was too late. Jo had put the telephone down.

I sat down at my desk sadly.

'Now what's going to happen?' I thought. 'Jo and his friend will come to see me. They'll ask me if I know where Elaine Garfield is. But I don't know where she is. I wonder if they will believe me when I tell them.'

The telephone rang again. I picked it up.

'Hello,' I said.

'Hello, Samuel,' said a familiar voice.

'Hello, Sergeant Murphy,' I replied, trying to sound pleased.

'We've just telephoned New York,' the sergeant said angrily, 'and the New York police were very helpful. The New York police told us that there is no such person as Helen Garfield. Helen Garfield does not exist. There is no one living in New York called Helen Garfield. You were lying when you told me that you were working for Helen Garfield.'

'But . . .' I started.

'Now, listen,' the sergeant interrupted, 'I am sending a police car round to your office. I want to see you. Wait for the police car. Don't go out.'

The sergeant put down the telephone and I sat back in my chair. I was worried. What would happen now? Jo was coming to see me and so was a policeman. I tried to think of what I would say to them both. I hoped that the policeman and Jo would not arrive at the same time.

18

I Find Elaine Garfield

The telephone rang again. I was afraid to answer it. The telephone continued ringing. Finally, I did answer it.

'Hello,' I said.

'Is that Mr Samuel?' asked a voice. It was Helen Garfield.

'Yes, Miss Garfield,' I replied, 'this is Len Samuel speaking.'

'I must see you,' said Helen Garfield.

'Well, I would like to talk to you, too, Miss Garfield,' I said slowly. 'I think there are a lot of things you and I must talk about.'

'Right,' the girl said, 'meet me at the "Seventh Mann" café in five minutes. Do you know where the café is? It's about half a mile from your office.'

'I know the "Seventh Man", 'I replied, 'but I can't meet you in five minutes, because I'm expecting visitors.'

'You must come at once, Mr Samuel,' she said.

'But . . .' I began.

It was too late. Helen Garfield had put her telephone down.

I got up from the chair and walked to the door. I decided to go and meet Helen Garfield. Both Jo and Sergeant Murphy had told me not to go out. But I decided I would rather talk to Helen Garfield than to the policeman or to Jo. If Jo and the policeman came when I was out, they could talk to each other.

I left the building and drove the Chrysler down the road. I was very lucky, because I was able to park right outside the "Seventh Mann". I walked into the café.

Helen Garfield was sitting at a table in the corner. I walked over and sat down beside her. I asked the waiter for a cup of coffee. I drank the coffee without saying anything. Then I put the cup down and looked at the beautiful, blonde girl sitting beside me.

'Miss Garfield,' I said, you are a very beautiful girl, but I think you are a liar. I think that everything you've said to me has been lies. I don't think you've ever told me the truth.'

The blonde girl's face slowly became red. She looked straight at me.

'Mr Samuel,' she said, 'I'm paying you a lot of money to work for me. I asked you to find my sister. I didn't ask you to call me a liar.'

'Well, Miss Garfield, I think I have found Elaine Garfield. Would you like me to tell you where she is?'

'Yes,' the blonde girl said, 'where is Elaine?'

'She's here in this café,' I said. 'Elaine Garfield is sitting next to me. You are Elaine Garfield. Helen Garfield doesn't exist. You pretended to be Helen Garfield, but there really never was any such person.

'The police in New York say that Helen Garfield doesn't exist,' I went on. 'Helen Garfield and Elaine Garfield are the same person. You are Elaine Garfield and you pretended to be Helen.'

The blonde girl stood up angrily.

'How much money do you want, Mr Samuel? You are no longer working for me,' she shouted.

'Sit down,' I said quietly.

The blonde girl did not sit down, so I pulled her down beside me.

'Now listen, Miss Garfield,' I said firmly. 'You are going to tell me all about yourself and why you came to see me. I want to know all about Benny Greep and Las Cabanas. I want to know why you disappeared.'

'I won't tell you anything,' she said.

'Oh, yes, you will tell me everything,' I replied, 'you'll tell me everything or else I'll take you straight to the police. You see, the police are looking for me at this moment.

'The police think that I may have killed Benny Greep,' I

continued. 'The police know that I had a fight at Las Cabanas last night. A red haired man and his tall friend are also chasing me. They are the two men who started the fight at Las Cabanas. They will try to kill me if I don't tell them where you are. So you see, Miss Garfield, I think you had better tell me everything. I'm the only person who can help you.'

The blonde girl sat in silence for a minute. Then she began to cry.

'All right,' she said, 'I'll tell you everything. I *am* Elaine Garfield.'

19

Everything Is Explained

I looked at the blonde girl.
'So you agree that you're really Elaine Garfield and not Helen,' I said quietly. 'Now tell me about Benny Greep.'

The girl took a deep breath.

'Suzy Graham and I used to go out dancing together a lot,' said Elaine. 'We often went to Las Cabanas. One night when we were there, I met a wonderful man called Benny. Benny was the drummer in the band. I liked him very much and went to the nightclub very often, to see Benny. We became very good friends.'

The girl stopped again and took out her handkerchief.

'Go on,' I said quietly.

'I used to go to Las Cabanas to see Benny nearly every night, but it was difficult for us to talk to each other,' the girl continued.

'Why was it difficult for you and Benny to talk to each other?' I asked.

'Because Benny was the drummer in the band, of course,'

Elaine Garfield replied. 'We couldn't talk to each other very much, because he was playing with the band most of the evening.'

'I understand,' I said and ordered two more coffees.

'So I spent a lot of time in Las Cabanas, watching Benny play the drums,' the girl said. 'And I also watched everything else which happened in the nightclub.'

'What did you see?' I asked.

'I didn't notice anything unusual at first,' the girl replied. 'But, after a few nights, I noticed that the same people always came to the club, at the same time.'

'Which people?' I asked.

'There was a red-haired man, a tall man who never took off his hat, and one or two others,' said Elaine Garfield.

'Yes,' I said, 'I think I have met two of them. They were the men who hit me on the head in the Manson Building.'

'Anyway,' the girl continued, 'one night, I asked Benny why these men came to the club every night. Benny told me not to ask questions. So I watched the men more carefully afterwards and noticed that they always arrived with bags. But when the men left, they weren't carrying bags.'

'What did you do then?' I asked.

'I asked Benny about the men again,' she said. 'Benny said that there were a lot of strange things happening at Las Cabanas, and that it was dangerous to ask questions.'

The waiter brought the coffees and Elaine waited until he had gone.

'One night,' she continued, 'one of the men was sitting at the table next to me. He was talking to some other men and he opened the bag that he was carrying. I was sitting quite close and I could see into the bag. The bag was full of diamonds and jewellery.'

'Really?' I said and drank my coffee.

'I told Benny about the bag of jewellery, later on in the evening,' continued Elaine. 'Benny was very excited at the news.

'The bag was full of diamonds and jewellery.'

He told me that he had known for a long time that criminals used Las Cabanas. They used the club as a place to buy and sell stolen things. Benny and I talked all evening about the bag of jewellery. Benny said that the jewellery was stolen. The men who were selling it were criminals and they had stolen the jewellery.

'Well,' Elaine continued, 'Benny wanted to steal one of the bags. He said that the jewellery was stolen, so it didn't matter if we stole it from the criminals. I agreed to help him. We hoped to sell the bag and to use the money to go away together.'

'I see,' I said, 'and did you help Benny to steal the bag of jewellery?'

'Yes, we waited for nearly a week,' Elaine replied. 'Then, last Sunday, I had a chance to steal the bag. It was at the end of the evening, and nearly everyone had left the club. I had found out where they hid the bag and I was able to take it and give it to Benny. Benny had big bags in which he carried his drums. It was easy for him to hide the bag of jewellery in the drum bag. We left the club together, with the bag of jewellery. We decided to hide the jewellery in my apartment and then sell it later.

'The next day was Monday,' Elaine continued, 'and I went to work. In the afternoon, I had a telephone call from Benny. Benny said that the red-haired man knew that the bag of jewellery had been stolen. He was very angry. Benny told me to stop work and go home. He told me to stay at home, to make sure that no one came to take the jewels. Benny was going to continue working at Las Cabanas. Then no one would think that he had stolen the jewels.'

'And did you stay at home?' I asked.

'Yes, I stayed at home for three days,' Elaine replied. 'But I was afraid that the red-haired man would find out where I was living. Then he would come to get the bag of jewellery.'

'So what did you do?' I asked.

'That was easy,' she said, with a smile. 'I moved into a hotel in the centre of the town and then came to see you.'

'But why did you come to see me?' I asked.

'To make sure that I was safe,' said Elaine. 'I pretended to be my sister and said that I had disappeared. I asked you to find me. Then I knew that I was safe.'

'Why?' I asked.

'Because you were looking for me,' Elaine continued. 'If the men from Las Cabanas found me or took me away, you would find out and chase them.'

'Thank you very much for thinking that I am such a good detective,' I said. 'But why didn't you tell me the truth?'

'That's easy,' said Elaine. 'I didn't want to tell you about the jewels.'

20

I'm Sorry, Mr Samuel

'Go on with your story,' I said.
'The evening I came to see you at your office,' said Elaine, 'I telephoned Benny at Las Cabanas. I told Benny what I had done. Benny told me that the red-haired man knew that we had stolen the jewellery. Benny told me that there would be no trouble if I brought the jewels back to Las Cabanas the next night.'

'You were stupid to trust the red-haired man,' I said.

'I know,' the girl said. 'I was afraid. So I asked you to meet me at Las Cabanas at half past eleven.'

'So you didn't know that Benny was dead until I told you at Las Cabanas,' I said.

'No,' Elaine said. 'That is why I ran away before midnight. I decided not to give them the jewellery, because they had killed Benny.'

'You've still got the jewels, then?' I asked, in surprise. 'Where are they?'

'Here,' Elaine said, and pointed to a small bag under the table.

I reached under the table, picked up the bag and opened it. The bag was full of diamonds and jewellery. Just then I heard a voice and, at the same time, Elaine screamed.

'Give it to me!' said the voice.

I looked up quickly and saw Jo standing beside me. His tall friend was right behind him.

'Give me the bag!' said Jo, once again.

'How did you know I was here?' I asked.

'You parked your car right outside,' said Jo, with a laugh. 'Now, give me the bag.'

I passed him the bag. As I gave him the bag, I jumped to my feet and hit Jo hard in the face. He tripped and fell heavily onto the floor. I moved towards the tall man, who was still standing a few feet away. I was about to run at him, but then I stopped. The tall man had taken a gun from his pocket and the gun was pointing straight at me.

'Right,' said the tall man. 'Don't move or else I'll shoot you.'

Jo got up from the floor. He still had the bag of jewellery in his hand. Together, Jo and his friend with the gun walked towards the door. They walked backwards, to make sure that Elaine and I did not try to get the bag back.

As the two men reached the door, I started to laugh.

'What are you laughing at?' shouted the man with the gun.

'Look behind you,' I said.

Both men turned around and looked. In the doorway of the café stood Sergeant Murphy, with two other policemen. Sergeant Murphy jumped on the tall man with the gun and Jo ran back into the café. I stepped forward to stop Jo and he ran straight into me. We both fell on the floor and the two policemen ran up. One of the policemen held Jo. The other policeman held me.

*I looked up quickly and saw Jo standing beside me. His tall
friend was right behind him.*

'They are the criminals,' I shouted, pointing at Jo and his friend, 'not me.'

'You are all coming down to the police station,' Sergeant Murphy said and looked over to Elaine Garfield. 'You must come, too.'

It took a long time to tell Sergeant Murphy the whole story. In the end, he believed what Elaine and I told him. The sergeant warned me not to tell him lies again, and agreed to let me go free. Elaine told Sergeant Murphy all she knew about Las Cabanas. The sergeant was very pleased to catch Jo and his friend with the jewels. Sergeant Murphy agreed to let Elaine go free, because she helped catch the criminals.

As we were leaving the police station, I asked Sergeant Murphy how he had found us in the "Seventh Man" café.

'It was very lucky, really,' said the sergeant. 'We went to your office to see you, but you weren't there. As we were leaving, we saw the red-haired man and his friend entering. We waited and when they left, we followed them to the café.'

'Thank you very much, Sergeant,' said Elaine. 'And thank you very much, Mr Samuel.'

'That's all right,' I said, 'you are paying me fifty dollars a day.'

'I'm sorry, Mr Samuel,' Elaine said, 'I'm afraid I can't pay you. Now that I've given the jewels to the police, I don't have any money.'

I smiled and got into the old grey Chrysler and drove back to the office. I didn't say goodbye. When I got back to the office, I sat down in my chair. It's not much fun being a private eye. You get hit on the head, nearly killed, and chased by the police. And you don't always get paid.

Shane *by Jack Schaefer*
Old Mali and the Boy *by D. R. Sherman*
Bristol Murder *by Philip Prowse*
Tales of Goha *by Leslie Caplan*
The Smuggler *by Piers Plowright*
The Pearl *by John Steinbeck*
Things Fall Apart *by Chinua Achebe*
The Woman Who Disappeared *by Philip Prowse*
The Moon is Down *by John Steinbeck*
A Town Like Alice *by Nevil Shute*
The Queen of Death *by John Milne*
Walkabout *by James Vance Marshall*
Meet Me in Istanbul *by Richard Chisholm*
The Great Gatsby *by F. Scott Fitzgerald*
The Space Invaders *by Geoffrey Matthews*
My Cousin Rachel *by Daphne du Maurier*
I'm the King of the Castle *by Susan Hill*
Dracula *by Bram Stoker*
The Sign of Four *by Sir Arthur Conan Doyle*
The Speckled Band and Other Stories by *Sir Arthur Conan Doyle*
The Eye of the Tiger *by Wilbur Smith*
The Queen of Spades and Other Stories *by Aleksandr Pushkin*
The Diamond Hunters *by Wilbur Smith*
When Rain Clouds Gather *by Bessie Head*
Banker *by Dick Francis*
No Longer at Ease *by Chinua Achebe*
The Franchise Affair *by Josephine Tey*
The Case of the Lonely Lady *by John Milne*

For further information on the full selection of
Readers at all five levels in the series, please refer
to the Macmillan Readers catalogue.

Published by Macmillan Heinemann ELT
Between Towns Road, Oxford OX4 3PP
Macmillan Heinemann ELT is an imprint of
Macmillan Publishers Limited
Companies and representatives throughout the world

ISBN 0 435 27245 4

First published 1975
Design and illustration © Macmillan Publishers Limited 1998, 2002
Heinemann is a registered trademark of Reed Educational & Professional Publishing Limited
This version first published 2002

Illustrated by John Richardson
Cover by Mark Olroyd and Threefold Design

Printed in China

2006 2005 2004 2003 2002
22 21 20 19 18 17 16 15 14 13